Listening to **Leaders**

Why Should I Listen to POLICE OFFICERS?

Christine Honders

PowerKiDS
press™

NEW YORK

Published in 2020 by The Rosen Publishing Group, Inc.
29 East 21st Street, New York, NY 10010

Editor: Greg Roza
Book Design: Rachel Rising

Photo Credits: Cover (insert) Sean Locke Photography/Shutterstock.com; Cover (background) Lia Koltyrina/Shutterstock.com;
pp. 5, 9 a katz/Shutterstock.com; p. 7 Bloomberg/Contributor/Getty Images; p. 11 kali9/E+/Getty Images; p. 13 Roman Tiraspolsky/Shutterstock.com; p.15 Richard Hutchings/Corbis Documentary/Getty Images; p. 17 photokup/Shutterstock.com; p. 19 Dan Holm/Shutterstock.com;
p. 21 Steve Debenport/E+/Getty Images; p. 22 LifetimeStock/Shutterstock.com.

Cataloging-in-Publication Data

Names: Honders, Christine.
Title: Why should I listen to police officers? / Christine Honders.
Description: New York : PowerKids Press, 2020. | Series: Listening to leaders | Includes glossary and index.
Identifiers: ISBN 9781538341766 (pbk.) | ISBN 9781538341780 (library bound) | ISBN 9781538341773 (6 pack)
Subjects: LCSH: Police--Juvenile literature.
Classification: LCC HV7922.H66 2019 | DDC 363.2--dc23

Manufactured in the United States of America

CPSIA Compliance Information: Batch #CSPK19 For further information contact Rosen Publishing, New York, New York at 1-800-237-9932.

Contents

It's the Law

Every place in the world has laws.
Laws are rules that tell people what
they are allowed to do. Police officers
are the people who **enforce** laws.
They keep us safe. They solve crimes.
They teach people how to protect
themselves. That's why you should
always listen to police officers.

Police Training

Police officers are trained at special schools called academies. They learn about laws. They're taught how to deal with emergencies. They learn how to **communicate** with people who need help. They're trained in driving safety and gun safety. They learn how to take care of you if you get hurt.

In Uniform

All officers wear a uniform. They also wear badges with their name on them. This is so people know who they are if they need help. Many officers in cities and towns drive police cars. But sometimes they ride bikes or fly in helicopters. Some police officers get around on horseback!

9

Crime Fighters

It's the officers' job to fight crime. They drive around neighborhoods and make sure everyone is **obeying** the laws. If they see a crime, they figure out the best way to stop it. They also help make sure the person breaking the laws gets punished.

Street Safety

Police officers stop people from speeding. They direct **traffic** on busy streets to keep accidents from happening. Sometimes they help kids cross the street on the way to school. Police officers make sure people follow traffic laws. This keeps everyone in the neighborhood safe when they're on the road.

13

Rescue Missions

Police officers are the first to respond when someone needs help. They know how to rescue people in emergencies. Officers want to protect you. They put themselves in danger to make sure you're safe. You should always call the police if you're a **victim** of a crime. They will help find out who was **responsible**.

Always Ready

Police officers are always ready to work. Officers **patrol** your neighborhood twenty-four hours a day. If you need a police officer, you can call 9-1-1 any time of day or night. Police officers give up time with their families and friends to make sure the **community** is safe.

Helping People

Police officers like to talk to the people in the community. They teach people how to stay safe at home and on the road. They remind people to call them if they see something that might be dangerous. They teach people to stay away from drugs and other things that can hurt them.

19

Protecting You

Police officers care about protecting kids. They come to schools to teach you how to keep yourself safe. They tell you to never, ever talk to strangers. They'll tell you how to find a police officer if you get lost. They'll show you how to call 9-1-1 in case of an emergency.

Heroes of the Community

Police officers aren't just part of the community. They're heroes of the community. They work many hours to make sure the laws are followed. They solve crimes. They help us when we are hurt. You should always listen to police officers. They make us safer every single day.

Glossary

communicate: To share ideas and feelings through sounds and motions.

community: The people living in a place, as well as the place itself.

enforce: To make sure something is done.

obey: To follow the rules or someone in charge.

patrol: To watch or guard something.

responsible: Having a duty to do something.

traffic: The vehicles, people, ships, or planes moving along a route.

victim: Someone who is hurt or fooled.

Index

C

crime, 4, 10, 14, 22

D

drugs, 18

E

emergencies, 6, 14, 20

L

laws, 4, 6, 10, 22

N

9-1-1, 16, 20

P

patrols, 16

T

training, 6

U

uniform, 8

V

victims, 14

Websites

Due to the changing nature of Internet links, PowerKids Press has developed an online list of websites related to the subject of this book. This site is updated regularly. Please use this link to access the list: www.powerkidslink.com/ltl/police